Made in the USA
Monee, IL
07 February 2021

59826215R10057